MW01698328

Nurturing the
Families of the World

UPDATED Nurturing Parenting Easy Reader Handbook

English Edition

Stephen J. Bavolek, Ph.D.
Illustrations by Cyndee Kaiser

Uniting the World's Families through Nurturing Parenting

Family Development Resources, Inc.
Publishers of the Nurturing Parenting Programs
800-688-5822   435-649-5822
NurturingParenting.com
AssessingParenting.com

CODE: NPER

ISBN # 1-57202-174-8
Printed in the United States of America

The *Nurturing Parenting Easy Reader Handbook* is based on the proven effectiveness of the validated family-based Nurturing Parenting Programs.®

For more information regarding the Nurturing Parenting Programs, Assessments and Inventories, and Training, contact:or more information, contact:

The Nurturing Parenting Programs
Family Development Resources, Inc.
800-688-5822 435-649-5822
FDR@NurturingParenting.com
NurturingParenting.com

Assessments and Inventories

For more information regarding valid and reliable inventories designed to assess parenting practices, beliefs, knowledge and skills, visit our website at **AssessingParenting.com**

Table of Contents
Updated Easy Reader Parent Handbook

About the Author

Stephen J. Bavolek, Ph.D. is a recognized leader in the fields of child abuse and neglect treatment and prevention, and parenting education. Born and raised in Chicago, Dr. Bavolek's professional background includes working with emotionally disturbed children and adolescents in schools and residential settings, and abused children and abusive parents in treatment programs. Dr. Bavolek has conducted extensive research in the prevention and treatment of child abuse and neglect.

He received his doctorate at Utah State University in 1978 and completed a post-doctoral internship at the Kempe Center for the Prevention and Treatment of Child Abuse and Neglect in Denver, Colorado. He has held university faculty positions at the University of Wisconsin - Eau Claire, and the University of Utah. Dr. Bavolek has received numerous international, national, state and local awards for his work, including induction in 1989 into the Royal Guild of the International Social Work Round Table in Vienna, Austria, and selection in 1983 by Phi Delta Kappa as one of 75 young educators in the country who represent the best in educational leadership, research and services. In addition, he was selected by Oxford Who's Who in 1993 as a member of the elite registry of extraordinary professionals and in 1998 as a member of the elite registry of extraordinary CEO's. Dr. Bavolek was also Mental Health Professional of the Year of Northern Wisconsin in 1985 and Child Advocate of the Year in Utah in 1991. In 1980, he was recognized by the Military Order of the Purple Heart for outstanding research and services to the handicapped.

Dr. Bavolek has conducted thousands of workshops, has appeared on radio and television talk show programs, and has published numerous books, articles, programs and newsletters. He is the principal author of the Nurturing Parenting Programs,® programs which treat and prevent child abuse and neglect, and the Adult-Adolescent Parenting Inventory (AAPI-2), an inventory designed to assess high risk parenting attitudes. Dr. Bavolek is President of Family Development Resources, Inc. and Executive Director of Family Nurturing Centers, International.

About the Illustrator

Cyndee Kaiser lives in Eau Claire, Wisconsin and is the mother of three grown children. They are the inspirations for many of the pictures in this book. Along with drawings, Ms. Kaiser is also a muralist and teacher. To see more examples of her work, go to www.cyndeekaiser.com.

Introduction to the Nurturing Parenting Easy Reader Handbook

Updated Version

Greetings! I'm Dr. Stephen Bavolek, principal author of the Nurturing Parenting Programs, and of the Easy Reader Nurturing Parenting Handbook. I'm pleased that you want to learn about the philosophy, practices and strategies of Nurturing Parenting. The book you have in your hand right now represents an updated version of the Easy Reader we first published in 2006. Since that initial publication, the Easy Reader has quickly become a very popular parenting manual nationwide. The purpose behind the Easy Reader is to help parents and other caregivers develop their understanding, knowledge and skills of Nurturing Parenting, a proven approach to helping families live in harmony and have fun together.

The English word "nurturing" comes from the old Latin word "nu tri tura" meaning to nurse, to nourish and to promote growth. And in our role as parents, isn't that the true meaning of the term "to parent"? Nurturing is a very powerful force on earth. Without nurturing, all forms of life couldn't exist. Simply, every person, plant or animal on earth needs to be nourished to live. And for human beings, nurturing the positive qualities in each child, teen and adult in our lives is perhaps the single most important thing all of us can do to live in harmony and happiness. Clearly, when nurturing is not present, it is easy to see how human beings can be cruel and inhumane.

To nurture is to promote the growth and development of all of one's positive traits, qualities and characteristics. To nurture is to respect and care for yourself, for other human beings, and for the environment. To nurture is to view the world and all the people, animals and things in it as having value and worth. As a parent, to nurture is to believe with all of your heart in the inherent goodness of your children.

The **Easy Reader** was developed to make nurturing parenting easy to understand and practice. The Updated Version has 50 chapters. The new chapters are: *Rating Nurturing Skills; Ages and Stages: Infants; Ages and Stages: Toddlers; Ages and Stages: Preschoolers; Ages and Stages: School-Aged Children; Skills Strips; Touching My Children and My Touch History; Child Proofing Your House From Danger; Feeding Your Children Nutritious Foods; STDs, Developing Children's Sexual Self-Worth; Ignoring as a Parenting Technique; the Dangers of Second Hand Smoke; and Communicating Thoughts and Feelings.* The practices presented in the Easy Reader have been proven over the years to work in raising healthy and caring kids. However, just like all practices that are meaningful, there are no quick fixes or short cuts, and no "technique" can substitute for a close and meaningful parent-child relationship.

The lessons in the Easy Reader address several major concepts:

1. **Nurturing as a Philosophy.** Presented are the basic foundations of nurturing as a philosophy of parenting, as well as a philosophy of life.
2. **Childhood Growth and Development.** A nurturing parent understands the importance of having appropriate developmental expectations of their children. Children need to experience success to improve their self worth. Recognizing that many parents have young children and children over the age of five, a chapter is devoted to understanding the developmental characteristics of school-age children.
3. **Discipline with Dignity.** Dignity means to treat another person honorably. Teaching and guiding children to be cooperative and contributing members of a family requires parents to behave dignified.
4. **Empathy.** The ability to be aware of, understand and respond appropriately to your children is the key in being a nurturing parent.
5. **Managing Feelings.** Recognizing and managing feelings is a basic quality of nurturing parenting.
6. **Communication.** Often identified as the major problem between parents and children, we address positive communication skills.
7. **Self-Worth and Empowerment.** A positive self worth is the foundation for treating others with respect and value. Teaching children to use their Personal Power in positive ways contributes to their overall positive Self-Worth as well as a positive and healthy Sexual Self-Worth.
8. **Making Good Choices and Keeping Kids Safe.** Smoking, drugs and alcohol use, sex, peer pressure are all issues that confront families daily.
9. **Nurturing Routines.** Children excel when their environment is predictable and nurturing.

In 1983, the Nurturing Program for Parents and their School Age Children was the first nationally published, validated parenting program designed for parents and their children to prevent child maltreatment through nurturing parenting. Today, there are Nurturing Parenting Programs for parents and children of different ages, abilities and nationalities. Programs and materials have been translated in different languages that are available to families throughout the world.

My sincerest wishes are extended to you and your family for a life filled with nurturing, love and happiness.

Stephen J. Bavolek, Ph.D.

Chapter 1
Nurturing Parenting

Attachment ...
unconditional love for
your children.

Empathy ...
taking care of your
children.

Nurturing Yourself ...
taking care of yourself.

Gentle Touch ...
holding, rocking and gently touching your children.

Expressing Feelings ...
helping your children express their feelings.

Discipline ...
teaching and guiding your children.

Expectations ...
helping your children succeed!

Try this ...
Discuss the "Nurturing Program" with your partner and other family members. Describe to them the seven areas of parenting the program will cover. What was their response?

Rating My Nurturing Skills

Use the chart below to rate your skills at the start and end of your program. Measure how much you have changed!

Directions:

Mark your responses in the columns **Start** when you begin the program. When you complete the program, you will again record your responses in each area in the column marked **End**.

Ratings:

1 = I need **lots** of improvement.
2 = I need **some** improvement.
3 = I have **average** skills in this area.
4 = I have **good** skills in this area.
5 = I have **really good** skills in this area.

	Start	End
Attachment Having unconditional love for your children	1 2 3 4 5	1 2 3 4 5
Empathy Helping your children meet their basic needs	1 2 3 4 5	1 2 3 4 5
Nurturing Yourself Finding time for yourself and taking care of yourself	1 2 3 4 5	1 2 3 4 5
Gentle Touch Holding, rocking, touching and massaging your children	1 2 3 4 5	1 2 3 4 5
Discipline Using techniques other than spanking or shouting to teach and guide your children	1 2 3 4 5	1 2 3 4 5
Expressing Feelings Recognizing and expressing your feelings in positive ways	1 2 3 4 5	1 2 3 4 5
Expectations Having appropriate expectations for yourself and your children	1 2 3 4 5	1 2 3 4 5

Chapter 2

Nurturing as a Lifestyle

Nurturing is the most powerful force on earth.

It means to promote,
nourish and support life.

All life needs to be
nurtured to exist.

Without nurturing,
there wouldn't be any life.

Nurturing Parenting means ...
to be respectful and helpful to your children by caring:

- How they are feeling
- What they are thinking
- Why they are behaving the way they are
- Responding in physically and emotionally HELPFUL ways

Abusive and Neglecting Parenting means ...
to be disrespectful and hurtful to your children by:

- NOT caring how they are feeling
- NOT caring what they are thinking
- NOT caring why they are behaving they way they are, and
- Responding in physically and emotionally HURTFUL ways

There are **FOUR TRAITS** to our personality that develop by the way we were treated in our childhood. These traits affect the quality of our life and the way we raise our children.

Our **NURTURED** Self ...

the ability we have to take care of ourselves, trust others, feel good about ourselves, and expect others to treat us with respect and value.

Our **NURTURING** Self ...

the ability we have to care about others and treat them with respect and value.

Our **VICTIM** Self ...

the ability we have to abuse and neglect ourselves, mistrust others, feel bad about ourselves, and expect others to mistreat us.

Our **PERPETRATOR** Self ...

the ability we have to mistreat others by disrespecting them, hurting them and not valuing them.

Try this ...

1. When you feel like you might start acting like a perpetrator, take 10 deep breaths. Breathe in calm; breathe out anger. Breathe in strength; breathe out weakness. Breathe in love; breathe out hurt.

2. Notice the traits of others, including your children. What did you learn?

Chapter 3

Critical Times for Children's Brain Development

At certain times in the life of children, parts of the brain that are responsible for certain functions need to be stimulated so the connection between brain cells can get stronger.

Here are some activities that you can do to build strong brain cell connections ...

Vision Development ...
Critical Time: Birth to Six Months

Hold your baby so she can look around.

Hang mobiles above your baby's bed so he can look at interesting shapes.

Decorate your baby's room with colorful objects.

Vocabulary and Speech Development ...

Critical Time: Birth to 3 Years

Talk to your child in full sentences.

Play with your child.

Read to your child.

Tell stories to your child.

Sing to your child.

Explain things you are doing even though your baby can't talk along with you. General conversation is good for your baby!

Emotional Development ...

Critical Time: Birth to 18 Months

Pick up your baby when he cries. Talk to him and comfort him

Have the same people in your baby's life everyday.

Babies love consistency!
Establish **Nurturing Parenting Routines.**

Logic and Math Development ...

Critical Time: 1 to 4 Years

Give children safe things to play with.

Explain the purpose of household items.

Explain cause and effect.

Try This ...
Help build your child's brain cell connections by doing the suggested activities.

WHAT EVERY CHILD NEEDS

Interaction with You ...
helps your children
learn.

Stable Relationships ...
help your children
handle their stress.

Gentle Touch ...
helps your children's
brains grow!

A Safe & Healthy Home ...
helps your children explore
their world.

Quality Care ...
helps your children
learn to care for
themselves
and others.

Self-Esteem ...
helps your children feel good
about themselves
and others.

Communication ...
helps your children
build their verbal
skills.

Reading ...
helps your children's
brains grow and
encourages your
children to read.

Play ...
helps your children
develop their
creativity and
imagination!

Music ...

teaches your children new skills
and expands their world.

Try This ...
Take time every day and play, read, dance, touch, talk and interact with your children. Every positive experience you have with your children is building a stronger and more capable brain and a positive self-worth!

How did you spend time with your children this week? ______________________

____

____

____

____

Chapter 4

Building Parent-Child Bonding and Attachment

The feeling of closeness between the parent and the child is called **Bonding**.

WAYS TO BOND WITH YOUR BABY

Touch your baby.
Touch is necessary for survival.

Talk to your baby.
She can recognize your voice.

Smile at your baby.
Smiling promotes love and happiness.

Respect your baby's cues.
Being aware of your baby's cues is called Attunement.

Look at your baby.
Babies communicate with their movements, sounds and facial expressions. These are called cues. What is your baby telling you?

Feed your baby.
Touch, talk and look at your baby when feeding him. Feeding is a special time to increase the bond between you and your baby.

Parent-Child Attachment

The positive bond that began at birth continues to develop as the child grows older. This long term bond is called Attachment.

Attachment sends the message "I am here for you and I care about you." Feelings of attachment are important in forming trust and security.

Attachment Disorders

Children who suffer abuse and neglect in the first three years of life usually experience degrees of attachment disorders. Behaviors associated with attachment disorders include:

- excessive tantrums
- need for control
- defiance
- depression
- manipulation, and
- an inability to experience close relationships

WAYS TO BUILD STRONG PARENT-CHILD ATTACHMENT

Play with your child,

Talk to your child.

Hold your child in times of sadness and happiness.

Massage your child.

Use Positive Discipline.

Read books with colorful pictures.

Have appropriate expectations.

Show interest in your child's day.

Try This ...
Practice the suggestions offered to increase the feelings of parent-child bonding and attachment. What did you do? What was your child's response?

Chapter 5

Ages & Stages: Appropriate Expectations

PHYSICAL DEVELOPMENT

Children get older and bigger.

Fine Motor Skills increase (using a fork, using scissors).

Gross Motor Skills increase (jumping, running, crawling).

INTELLECTUAL DEVELOPMENT

Children learn more as they get older.

Children begin to figure out problems.

Children recognize shapes and colors, and say the alphabet.

LANGUAGE DEVELOPMENT

Children's communication skills increase.

Language expands from a few words to thousands of words.

Children use words and phrases in sentences.

Children communicate their needs and begin to understand the needs of others.

SOCIAL & EMOTIONAL DEVELOPMENT

Children's emotional growth goes from an early stage of dependence to a later stage of independence.

Try this ...

Keep a diary of how your children are changing. Daily and weekly observations and stories are fun to read to your children as they get older.

Chapter 6

Developmental Stage: INFANCY

The first year of an infant's life is exciting.

Babies can experience things that we just didn't think they could!

Did you know that babies can recognize their mother by her smell when the baby is only 6 to 10 days old?

At two weeks, babies will look at their own mother more than they will look at strangers.

As babies grow older during their first year of life, their body language, social interactions and intelligence also develop.

PHYSICAL DEVELOPMENT

Since the infant is pretty helpless at birth, he is totally dependent on parents and other adults for survival.

At around two months, a baby will ...

... Suck their fingers.

... Lift their head when on their stomach.

... Use their eyes to follow you.

... Be starting to teethe.

INTELLECTUAL DEVELOPMENT

The child learns about the world by ...

... Exploring objects.

Moving
around, and ...

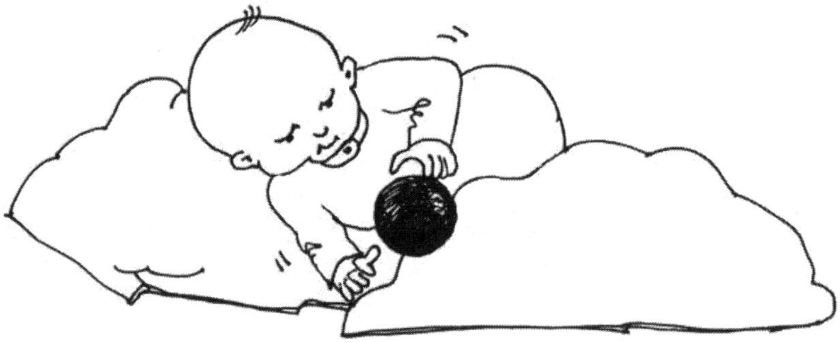

...Through the interactions
with her parents.

LANGUAGE DEVELOPMENT

Language develops very slowly during the first year.

By the end of the first year, the baby has about 2 to 8 words.

Babies communicate their needs without words. Crying is one way babies let their parents know they need something.

By the second month, babies begin cooing which is a way they show their pleasure.

Babbling begins between months 4 and 5.

It is very important for parents to talk to their babies so they can develop their language.

SOCIAL AND EMOTIONAL DEVELOPMENT

The first year babies are learning to develop trust or mistrust with themselves or others.

Infants love to be played with.

Infants like to be picked up and held.

At about 7 months, your baby may become attached to a favorite toy.

At 8 to 10 months, babies express frustration through crying.

At 12 months, babies love an audience and will repeat a behavior over and over.

Try this ...
Write down one behavior you noticed your baby doing in each of the four primary areas of development: physical, intellectual, language and social/emotional and share them with other family members.

Chapter 7

Developmental Stage: TODDLER

Toddlers can be intense, busy, curious and sometimes stubborn. Parenting a toddler is seldom dull.

This stage in life is often called the "Terrible Twos" because toddlers like to explore and gain control of their surroundings.

Toddlers are in a hurry to gain independence and enjoy life.

PHYSICAL DEVELOPMENT

Toddlers grow at a rapid rate.

At the end of the first year. The average one year old is 27-29 inches tall and weighs around 22 pounds.

By the end of the third year, the average three year old is 36 inches tall and weighs 35 pounds.

The toddler should ...

Be walking better without holding arms up for balance ...

... Be able to pick up things from a standing position.

... Like to push or pull toys.

... Be able to seat self in chair.

SMALL MUSCLE DEVELOPMENT (Fine Motor)

Combines use of several objects like using one object to hit another.

Begins to use spoon to eat.

Drinks from a cup.

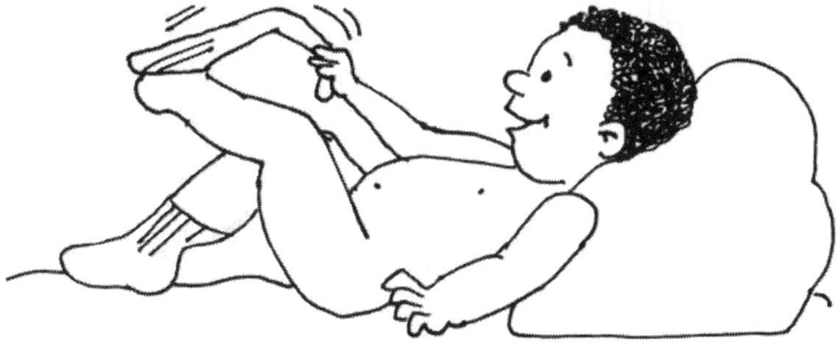

Removes shoes, socks and pants.

Builds a tower.

INTELLECTUAL DEVELOPMENT

Around 18 months, the toddler begins to understand that objects are independent from him and explores how these objects work.

The toddler also learns that the object remains the same no matter how he looks at it. This is called object permanence.

Language and memory occur around two years. By three years, children can remember people and events.

Toddlers are curious about textures.

Toddlers respond to directions: "Give me the block."

Toddlers can recognize themselves in a mirror.

LANGUAGE DEVELOPMENT

Says first meaningful words (12-24 months).

Toddler likes to talk to self.

Joins words together around 24 months.

Asks what and where questions (24-36 months).

SOCIAL AND EMOTIONAL DEVELOPMENT

Toddlers are active explorers and parents need to baby-proof the house.

Toddlers usually get upset when they have to separate from their moms.

Toddlers become more self-aware, more assertive and more independent. "NO" becomes a common word.

Somewhere between 18 to 24 months, toddlers are ready to learn potty training.

Try This ...
Write down one behavior you noticed your toddler doing in each of the four primary areas of development: physical, intellectual, language and social/emotional and share them with other family members.

Chapter 8

Developmental Stage: PRESCHOOLER

Between the ages of 3 to 6 years, the preschooler reaches out to the world for new experiences, friends and accomplishments.

LARGE MUSCLE DEVELOPMENT (Gross Motor)

Takes longer steps when running and walking.

Catches large ball.

Hops on one foot.

SMALL MUSCLE DEVELOPMENT (Fine Motor)

Can draw, use scissors and begin to color.

Can begin to read.

Copies shapes.

Can paint with broad strokes.

INTELLECTUAL DEVELOPMENT

This is the period of functional language by learning objects and people with symbols.

Asks a lot of questions about names of objects and activities *"What is that?"*

Asks questions about purpose: *"Why does it rain?"*

LANGUAGE DEVELOPMENT

Vocabulary grows from 900 words at three years to 2,000 words between 5 and 6 years.

By the age of five, uses complete sentences.

Uses "because, how and why" to interpret cause and effect.

Children love to giggle with "toilet talk."

SOCIAL/EMOTIONAL DEVELOPMENT

Children are highly social and want to play with other children.

Children initiate activities due to the need to gain mastery.

If children are made to feel stupid or silly about their activities, feelings of guilt can develop that last a lifetime.

Children play and have imaginary friends.

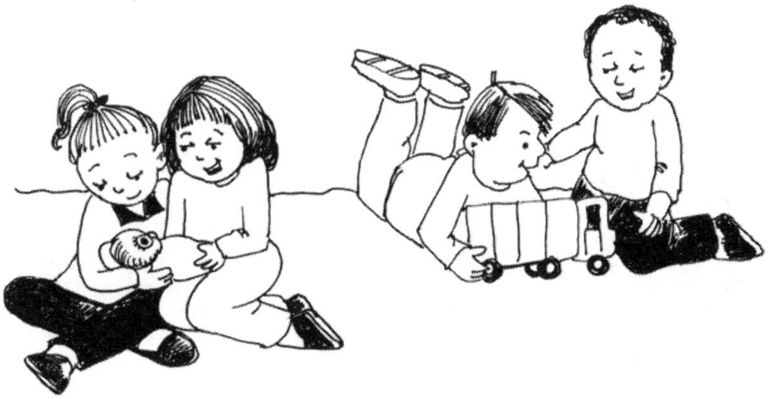

Most preschooler boys play with boys and girls play with girls around the age of 6 yrs.

Night time wetting can occur.

Fears can develop about monsters and scary people.

Masturbation is normal.

Try this ...
Write down one behavior you noticed your preschooler doing in each of the four primary areas of development: physical, intellectual, language and social/emotional and share them with other family members.

Chapter 9

Developmental Stage: SCHOOL-AGE

Children have new experiences and new friendships that are outside the family.

Many children 6 to 12 years will share their experiences if their parents are willing to listen.

Children learn during this period how to deal with success and failure; how to defend themselves from bullies and how to interact with adults.

PHYSICAL DEVELOPMENT

From ages 5 to 10 years, boys and girls have approximately the same height, weight and physical measurements.

By age 10 girls begin to mature physically more rapidly than boys.

INTELLECTUAL DEVELOPMENT

At around 6 years, children are able to figure out problems and give reasons for what they think.

At around 12 years, a child begins to think logically. He can draw conclusions, test ideas and think of possible alternatives to problems (skills needed in school).

LANGUAGE DEVELOPMENT

Vocabulary grows steadily each year. Sentence structure, grammar and meanings of words are the skills the child continues to develop and use.

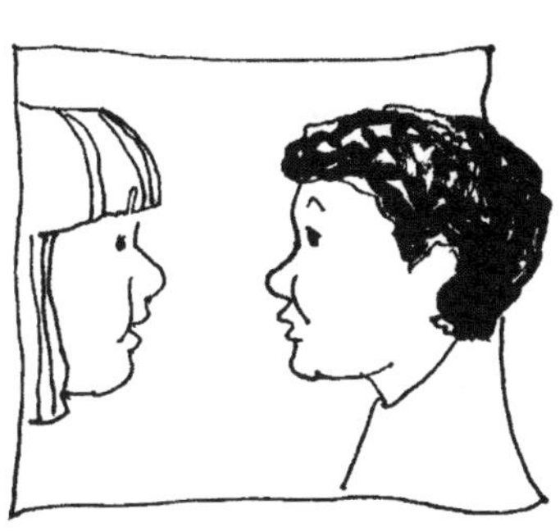

SOCIAL AND EMOTIONAL DEVELOPMENT

When parents encourage a child to make, do, or build things and reward their efforts, a sense of accomplishment is achieved.

When a child's efforts are discouraged or ridiculed, a sense of inferiority develops.

Homework becomes an issue.

A child's school experiences influence whether a child feels adequate or inferior.

Peers are the most important source of social contact.

Children participate in group activities to test their skills.

Feelings of inferiority, the result of not being encouraged by parents to participate in activities with peers, and learn new skills will affect the child in later stages of development.

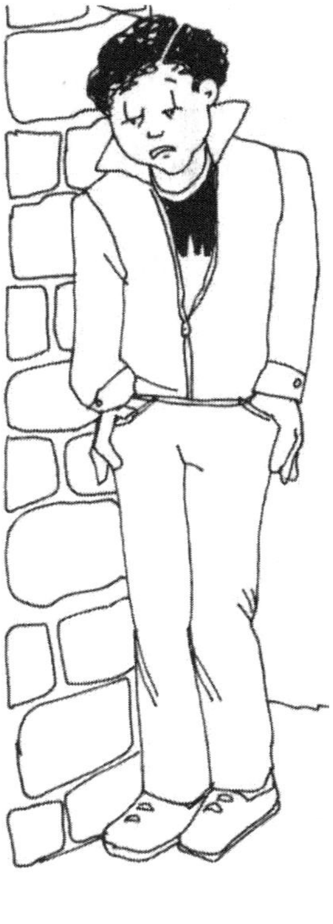

Children should be required to participate in household chores. This increases the child's sense of responsibility and self-worth.

Try this ...
Write down one behavior you noticed your school-age child doing in each of the four primary areas of development: physical, intellectual, language and social/emotional and share them with other family members.

Chapter 10
Skills Strips

Directions: Match the skill (behavior) with the correct age period. Circle the age you think children should be able to begin to perform the behaviors.

Behaviors	Age of Child				
	0 – 12 months	*12 – 24 months*	*24 – 36 months*	*36 – 48 months*	*48– 60 months*
1. Takes a few steps without support.	A	B	C	D	E
2. Repeats same syllable 2-3 times.	A	B	C	D	E
3. Builds tower of three blocks.	A	B	C	D	E
4. Says five different words.	A	B	C	D	E
5. Points to three body parts on self.	A	B	C	D	E
6. Uses pincer grasp to pick up object.	A	B	C	D	E
7. Imitates peek-a-boo.	A	B	C	D	E
8. Pulls off socks.	A	B	C	D	E
9. Holds and drinks from cup using 2 hands	A	B	C	D	E
10. Follows rules by imitating actions of other children.	A	B	C	D	E
11. Snaps or hooks clothing.	A	B	C	D	E
12. Pedals tricycle five feet.	A	B	C	D	E
13. Attempts to help parent with tasks by doing part of a chore (e.g. holds dustpan).	A	B	C	D	E
14. Walks backwards.	A	B	C	D	E
15. Will be attentive for five minutes while a story is read.	A	B	C	D	E
16. Sucks liquid from glass using a straw.	A	B	C	D	E
17. Imitates counting to three.	A	B	C	D	E
18. Puts on mittens.	A	B	C	D	E
19. Holds up fingers to tell age.	A	B	C	D	E
20. Uses word for bathroom need.	A	B	C	D	E
21. Stands on one foot for 4-8 seconds.	A	B	C	D	E
22. Uses words: sister, brother, grandmother.	A	B	C	D	E
23. Stays dry all night.	A	B	C	D	E
24. Takes turn with 8-9 other children.	A	B	C	D	E
25. Draws a man (Head, trunk, four limbs).	A	B	C	D	E
26. Engages in socially acceptable behavior in public.	A	B	C	D	E

Chapter 11
Male & Female Brain

Scientists are now discovering that the brain of a male is different from the brain of a female.

- Both the male and female brains have about 27 billion brain cells that form connections called networks. The more activity that is associated with a certain part of the brain, the more networks are made and the stronger they get.

- If certain parts of the brain are not used, the cells will weaken and dry up. The brain is a "use it or lose it" organ.

- Male and female brains produce hormones that support brain growth. The male hormone is called testosterone and the female hormone is called estrogen.

- If the child in the womb is a chromosomal male child (XY), the mother's hormonal system reads this as male and sends more testosterone. If the child is a chromosomal female (XX), the mother's hormonal system sends more female hormones.

- In the womb, the hormones are responsible for males and females developing their sexual organs and other gender specific traits.

- Brain development of all babies, no matter what their sex, is stimulated by all hormones.

- Male babies get more testosterone and develop a "male brain" while female babies get more estrogen and develop a "female brain".

- The development of the male and female brain in the womb can be affected by the stress the mother experiences during pregnancy.

- It's possible for a boy to get more estrogen and have a "female brain" and a girl to get more testosterone and have a "male brain." A lot of people experience sexual identity confusion.

- Remember: all males have some estrogen; all females have some testosterone.

MALE AND FEMALE BRAIN QUIZ

1. **Males would rather work on a project than talk.**
   True. More cortical areas in the male brain than in the female brain are devoted to the development of spatial skills like mechanical design, measurement and manipulation of physical objects.

2. **Males would prefer to read a book rather than play football or video games.**
   False. Since the male brain is devoting more cortical areas to spatials, less cortical areas are devoted to word use or production. In females, it's just the opposite.

3. **Males tend to talk less often and use fewer words than females.**
   True. The bundle of nerves that connects the right and left hemispheres of the brain is called the "corpus callosum." The corpus callosum is 24% smaller in males, resulting in males not connecting as many feelings or thoughts to words.

4. **Females act more impulsively than males.**
   False. The male brain secretes less serotonin than the female brain. Serotonin is the brain chemical that acts to calm us down.

5. **Males tend to be more aggressive than females.**
   True. This is due largely to lower levels of oxytocin in the male brain. Oxytocin is the brain chemical that helps us to be able to bond and demonstrate more empathy. The higher the level of oxytocin in the brain, the less aggressive the person is likely to be and more likely to link bonding and empathy in the verbal centers of the brain.

6. **Females and males bond differently.**
   True. Males rely more on "spatials" like playing basketball; females prefer to talk, relying more on "verbals." Bonding and attachment is influenced by hormones. Mothers have higher levels of oxytocin, which has been called "the nurturing hormone." When a woman is around small, helpless beings - babies, puppies, etc. there is a spike in this chemical. Fathers have much lower levels of oxytocin and therefore must bond and attach in different ways - socially, emotionally and psychologically.

7. **Males tend to be more patient than females.**
   False. Men take action first, talk second. Women are just the opposite. Lower levels of serotonin and oxytocin in the male brain are responsible for this trait. The male brain responds more quickly to obvious signals in action. Men are less inclined to stop, be patient, listen and communicate emotions verbally.

8. **Males have a stronger sex drive than females.**
   True. Men have a hormonal system that is dominated by testosterone. Testosterone is the sex and aggression hormone. Males have up to 20 times more testosterone than women.

9. **Males tend to zone out more than females.**
   True. Women's brains are constantly working. Whereas the male brain zones out and takes mental naps. Research shows that there is 15% more blood flow in the female brain than in the male brain.

10. **Males tend to solve problems by talking. Females tend to solve problems with action.**
    False. Males and females respond differently to problem situations. It's due to the way their brains operate. Males have "action oriented" empathy. Men are doers; they like to solve problems with action. Females express more of "feelings oriented" empathy. Women like to process feelings first, then work on solving problems.

Taken from "What Could He Be Thinking?" by Michael Gurian, St. Martin's Press, NY 2003.

Chapter 12

Empathy

Empathy is the ability of parents to care about their children.

Parents with Empathy ...
help their children get their needs met.

Parents with Empathy ...
try to figure out what their children are feeling.

Parents with Empathy ...
hold and rock their children when they need to be comforted.

Parents with Empathy ...
try to understand what their children are thinking.

Parents with Empathy ...
respond to their children in a caring way.

Try This ...
Children learn empathy from watching their parents and from the way their parents treat them. Develop a plan for building empathy by completing the following statements:

1. Things I can do to model empathy are: ________________________________

____

____

2. One non-empathic behavior I do that I definitely want to stop is: ______________

____

and instead I will________________________________

HELPING CHILDREN DEVELOP EMPATHY

Use nurturing ways to discipline your children.

Teach children to share their feelings.

Honor your children's feelings and desires.

Model empathy.

Teach children to take responsibility.

Develop morals ... teach children right from wrong.

Observe the good and bad behavior of others.

Develop Family Rules.

Teach children to notice non-verbal behavior.

Have children care for plants and pets.

Teach children to share.

Try this ...

Things I can do to help my children develop empathy are: ______________________

____

____

____

____

____

____

Chapter 13

The Needs of Adults and Children

The SPICES of Life

Social ...

The need to be with others.

Physical ...

The need for food, exercise, sleep.

Intellectual ...

The need to learn; the need for new ideas.

Creative ...

The need for dance, art, poetry, self-expression.

Emotional ...

The need to love and be loved.

Spiritual ...

The need to find meaning in life.

Try this ...

1. Using a scale from 0 to 3, rate each need area:

0 = Not Met; 1 = Low; 2 = Average; 3 = High

Need	**Rating** (Circle one for each need)
Social	0 1 2 3
Physical	0 1 2 3
Intellectual	0 1 2 3
Creative	0 1 2 3
Emotional	0 1 2 3
Spiritual	0 1 2 3

2. What I can do to get my needs met: ______________________________

____

____

____

Chapter 14

Recognizing and Understanding Feelings

Being able to recognize, express and understand emotions is one of the greatest traits of being a human being. Yet, we are taught throughout life that expressing emotions is not always a good thing.

As parents we want to raise our children to be emotionally healthy and to be able to express how they feel.

HERE ARE SOME GUIDELINES TO FOLLOW:

#1

All feelings have energy. The goal is to express our feeling energy appropriately.

#2

Learning not to express our feelings means learning to keep all our feeling energy inside.

#3

Keeping our feeling energy inside will sooner or later lead to problems.

#4

All emotions are good. It is the **way** the feeling energy is expressed that make feelings either good or bad.

#5

Avoid calling feelings "good" or "bad." Instead, use words like "comfort" and "discomfort" to describe feelings.

#6

Model appropriate ways to express your feelings.

As adults, our goal is to appropriately manage and express our feelings so our children can learn to appropriately manage and express their feelings.

Try this ...
When you have a feeling, give it a name. Make friends with all your feelings especially the ones that "get you in trouble and you can't control." By making friends, you can allow the feeling to be expressed safely and stay in control.

Chapter 15

Helping Children Handle Their Feelings

Here are some tips for helping your children handle their feelings ...

#1
Let children know that feelings are okay.

#2
Label the feeling you see or think you see.

#3

Encourage your children to talk about how they are feeling.

#4

Ask questions but don't tell children not to feel that way.

#5

Brainstorm what, if anything can be done.

#6

Honor children's desires.

#7

Teach children appropriate ways to express their feelings energy.

#8

PRAISE your children when they express their feelings appropriately!

Try this ...

Use the steps listed in the chapter to help your children be able to express and manage their feelings.

Chapter 16
Spoiling Your Children

Babies depend on parents to get their needs met. We call these **BASIC DEPENDENCY NEEDS.** Being fed, held, comforted, changed, played with and talked to are just some of these needs.

As babies grow into toddlers, preschoolers and beyond, their skills and abilities increase along with their desire to do more things for themselves. We call this **AUTONOMY**.

When children aren't encouraged to develop their autonomy, they continue to act like babies even though they are older.

This behavior is called **SPOILED**.

TO PREVENT "SPOILING" YOUR CHILDREN, TRY THE FOLLOWING:

#1 Encourage children to do things for themselves.

#2 Set appropriate guidelines and limits.

#3 Be consistent.

#4 Teach children to use words.

#5 Ignore whining.

#6 Hold children when they need comforting, but also hold them when they don't.

#7 Leave your children with other trusted adults for brief periods of time.

#8 Take time to nurture yourself alone, or with other adults.

Try this ...
Do things to promote your child's autonomy. What did you try? What was the result?

Chapter 17
Building Self-Worth

Self-Worth is the value people have for themselves.

It combines our **Self-Concept** (our ***thoughts*** of our self).

and our **Self-Esteem** (our ***feelings*** about our self).

Self-worth plays an important role in the way people behave. Generally, people with a positive self-worth treat themselves and others with respect.

People with a negative self worth generally don't think and feel positively about themselves and find it very difficult to treat others respectfully.

HERE ARE SOME TIPS TO IMPROVE THE SELF-WORTH OF CHILDREN:

#1

Put children in situations where they can succeed.

#2

Expect children to succeed and not fail at tasks.

#3

When children don't succeed at tasks, find out why.

#4

Use **"Praise for Doing"** statements to acknowledge accomplishments and efforts.

#5

Share your children's accomplishments and efforts in the presence of others.

#6

Be a good role model and praise yourself for your accomplishments and efforts.

#7

Avoid **Negative Labels**
for your children like
"lazy" or "stupid" ...

... Use only
Positive Labels
that improve
self-worth -
not damage it.

#8

Show respect for your children's feelings and opinions even though you don't agree with them.

#9

Have a special plate or cup at dinner time that is awarded to a family member for their efforts or accomplishments.

#10

Lastly, use terms like "Thanks for cooperating!" or "I appreciate your help!" to let children know that you are pleased with their behavior.

Try this ...
Use the ideas presented to improve your children's self-worth. What did you try? What happened?

Chapter 18
Personal Power

PERSONAL POWER is the life force or energy all people have to get their needs met. We can use our personal power in positive or negative ways.

Negative use of our personal power means we do things to meet our needs in ways that are self destructive or destructive to others.

Positive use of personal power means we do things to meet our needs that build our self-worth and the self-worth of others.

CONTROL is the use of our personal power to influence the behavior of others.

Positive Control means we do things for others that they can't do for themselves, like parents taking care of babies.

Negative Control means we take over and do things for others that they could do for themselves, like parents constantly telling children how to dress, what to eat, how to behave.

Power Struggles between parents and children occur when children feel they have no control or influence in their own lives. When parents are over-controlling, power struggles are sure to occur.

By controlling their children's lives, parents are taking power away from them. In turn, children are fighting to get their power back.

The goal is to help children use their power and control to make smart choices and lead healthy lives.

SOME SUGGESTIONS TO REDUCE POWER STRUGGLES ARE:

- Negotiate and compromise with your children.
- Problem solve and encourage children to come up with some solutions.
- Teach children to take responsibility for their behavior.
- Take ownership of your feelings and don't blame children for how you feel.
- Be fair, consistent and follow through on commitments.
- As parents, make sure to find time to nurture yourself.

Try this ...
Practice ways to use your personal power in positive ways. What did you do?
Practice ways to reduce power struggles with your children. What did you do?

Chapter 19
Discipline with Dignity

Discipline ...
means to teach like a
teacher instructs
her students.

Discipline ...
means to guide like the
shepherd guides
his sheep.

DISCIPLINE WITH DIGNITY ...
MEANS TEACHING AND GUIDING
YOUR CHILDREN WITH RESPECT!

A parent first establishes discipline when their children are very young.

Discipline ...
means setting boundaries and limits so children can learn right from wrong.

Parents have to guide and teach their young children so they will be safe.

As children get older, they work with parents in setting up rules that will guide and teach them and keep them safe.

The long-term goal of discipline is to guide and teach children right from wrong so they can make good, healthy choices throughout life.

Discipline does NOT mean being harsh and uncaring.

The word "harsh" comes from an old Scandinavian word that means "smelly and rotten."

When parents are being harsh, they are behaving smelly and rotten.

Children don't want to be around parents who are harsh - and will avoid them.

Teaching Children by hitting them or yelling at them is **NOT** discipline ...

... that is **VIOLENCE** and violence is not guidance.

Be the parent you would like raising **YOU** if you were your child.

Treat children the way you would like to be treated.

TO TEACH AND GUIDE YOUR CHILDREN TO BEHAVE POSITIVELY, FOLLOW THESE GUIDELINES ...

The time you spend with your children needs to be positive "time-in" for "time-out" to be effective.

Have age-appropriate expectations for your children.

Children are not small adults and need to experience success to feel good about themselves.

Children who feel good about themselves almost always feel good about others.

Model the behaviors you want your children to have. Children learn a lot by watching!

Parents need to be flexible and consistent. Inflexible parents can break.

Inconsistent parents are like a broken compass – they can't guide children properly because they keep changing directions.

Remember to take care of yourself and to get your adult needs met.

Parents who don't take care of themselves won't find parenting fun.

Try this ...

1. Identify two things you like about the way you discipline your children: __________

____

2. Identify two things you dislike about the way you discipline your children: ______

____

3. What can you do to improve? ______________________

____

Chapter 20
Why Parents Spank Their Children

Hitting children is an age old practice that is known to cause children physical and emotional harm.

Today we also know that repeated hitting prohibits the growth of healthy brain development.

SOME COMMON REASONS WHY PARENTS HIT THEIR CHILDREN:

Parents hit children ...

... because parents were hit when they were children.

Parents hit children...

... to teach them right from wrong.

Parents hit children ...
... **as a form of Punishment.**

Parents hit children ...
... **as an act of love.**

Parents hit children ...
... to teach children respect.

Parents hit children ...
... based on religious scriptures.

Parents hit children ...
... as a cultural practice.

Parents hit children ...

... when they are angry and lose control.

Parents hit children ...

... to prepare children for the "real world."

Try this ...

Take time to understand why you use spanking as a way of punishing children. Reflect back on the times that you were spanked as a child. Did your parents use the same reason for spanking you as you are using for spanking your children?

Chapter 21

Family Morals and Values

Morals ...

are beliefs we have about right and wrong and good and bad.

Without morals, people of all ages wouldn't know what to do and what not to do.

There are lots of ways children learn right from wrong, but the most powerful is ... from their **PARENTS**.

Children learn their morals from their parents, brothers and sisters, other family members, their friends, from the lessons taught in school and church, and from TV and movies.

Values ...

are the morals that family members practice on a regular basis.

When something has worth, it has value.

Values are **Morals** that have **Worth!**

What values
do your family have?

Try this ...
Make a list of the morals and values you have in your family.

Chapter 22

Family Rules

Family Rules ...
help everyone know what
is expected of them to
live in harmony
as a family.

Family Rules ...
are the guidelines that
children and family
members need to help
them practice their
morals and values.

Family Rules ...
involve EVERYONE!

EVERYONE gets to
have a say in making
Family Rules!

Values ...

are the morals that family members practice on a regular basis.

When something has worth, it has value.

Values are **Morals** that have **Worth!**

What values do your family have?

Try this ...

Make a list of the morals and values you have in your family.

Chapter 22
Family Rules

Family Rules ...
help everyone know what is expected of them to live in harmony as a family.

Family Rules ...
are the guidelines that children and family members need to help them practice their morals and values.

Family Rules ...
involve EVERYONE!

EVERYONE gets to have a say in making Family Rules!

Family Rules ...
have **DOs** and **DON'Ts**

DOs help family members learn what TO do.

DON'Ts help family members learn what NOT to do.

MAKING FAMILY RULES

#1

Get EVERYONE to participate.

#2

Get a large sheet of paper and a marker.

#3

Draw a line down the center of the paper.

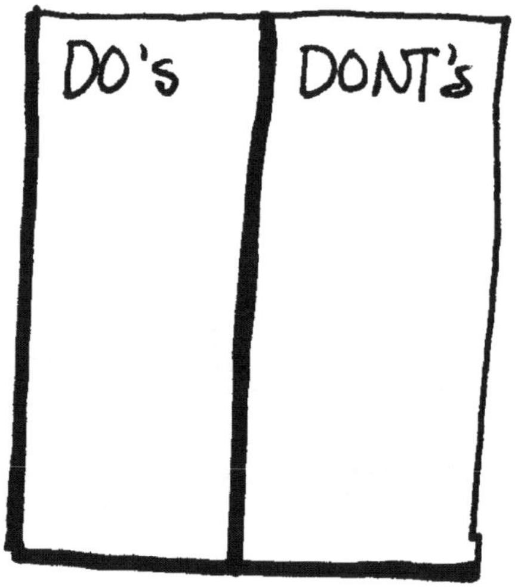

#4

Label one side **DOs**.
Label the other side **DON'Ts**.

#5

Share problem behaviors.

#6

Make a list of rules – for every DON'T, make sure you have a DO rule.

#7

Keep rules simple and clear.

#8

Limit rules to about 5 – 7.

#9

Hold family meetings to review the rules.

Try this ...

1. Bring your family together and make a list of Family Rules.

2. Make sure you have **DO** rules for all of your **DON'T** rules.

Chapter 23
Rewards & Punishments

A **Reward** is a consequence that helps teach and guide children to behave properly.

Rewards are a necessary part of discipline to guide and teach children right from wrong.

A **Reward** lets children know they have pleased their parents.

THERE ARE FIVE MAJOR TECHNIQUES THAT WORK WELL AS REWARDS ...

#1 PRAISE

Telling children
they are special is
Praise for "BEING!"

~ or ~

Telling children you like
their behavior is
Praise for "DOING!"

#2 NURTURING TOUCH

Gentle hugs, back rubs, holding and gently rocking your child are all nurturing touches!

#3 PRIVILEGES

Staying up a little later, extra time watching TV or playing video games, or an extra story before bed time are all privileges.

#4 OBJECTS

Almost anything ranging from stickers to toys can be object rewards.

#5 ALLOWANCE

Use allowance with older children for the purpose of teaching them how to manage money.

Try this ...

1. Use praise and touch as daily rewards for your children.
2. On special occasions, use privileges and objects as rewards for your children.
3. Where appropriate, use allowance as a reward for older children.

Using Punishments to Guide Children

Punishment ...
is a negative consequence that helps teach and guide children to behave appropriately.

NEVER ... hit a child!

NEVER ... yell at a child!

NEVER ... punish babies!

HERE ARE FIVE TYPES OF PUNISHMENT THAT WORK WELL ...

TIME-OUT ...
is being alone
for a <u>brief</u> period
of time.

BEING GROUNDED ...
is being confined
to the yard or home
for a <u>brief</u> period
of time.

DISAPPOINTMENT FROM PARENTS ...
is a statement or look of concern.

PAY BACK ...
If you make a mess, you clean it up.

LOSS OF A PRIVILEGE ...

If you misuse a privilege, you lose it and need to earn it back.

Try this ...
Use the punishments presented in this chapter as a way of guiding children and teaching them right from wrong.

Chapter 24
Praising Children and Their Behavior

Praise is a verbal or non-verbal way of letting children know how proud parents are of them or their efforts.

Praise can be ...

...a compliment,

... a facial expression,

... or a form of gentle touch.

RESEARCH SHOWS THAT CHILDREN WHO ARE PRAISED OFTEN ...

... have a positive self-worth,

... treat others in a positive way,

... are more popular in school,

... get better grades,

... and feel good because they pleased their parents!

THERE ARE TWO TYPES OF PRAISE ...

Praise for **BEING** and Praise for **DOING**

Praise for **"BEING"** lets children know parents value them for **who they are**!

Praise for **"DOING"** lets children know parents value them for **what they do**.

Use Praise for **BEING** and **DOING** separately.

Don't put the two types together!

Saying, "I really love you because you try so hard" lets children think you only love them when they try hard.

STEPS IN PRAISING:

1. Focus your attention on the child.
2. Move close to the child, if possible.
3. Try to get on the child's level.
4. Gently touch your child.
5. Look pleasant.
6. Offer your praise.
7. Offer a hug.

Try this ...
Use Praise and Gentle Touch each day with each of your children.

Chapter 25

Touching My Children and My Touch History

Touch is the most powerful of all interactions between a parent and a child.

THERE ARE THREE KINDS OF TOUCH:

Nurturing Touch
Rubs, pats, massages, hugs.

Hurting Touch
Spankings, scrapes, cuts, operations, rapes, attacks, broken bones, etc.

Scary Touch
Unwanted sexual touch, threats of hurting touch ("I'm gonna break your neck!").

Nurturing Touch has immediate positive and comforting effects.

Babies who regularly receive nurturing touch show increased weight gain, improved body tone, alertness and consolability.

The Nurturing Parent uses nurturing touch only. Research tells us that Nurturing touch decreases stress and depression. It is one of the greatest gifts we can give our children.

Try this ...
Practice giving nurturing touch to your children every day. Hug them, hold them, play with them, cuddle with them. A strong parent-child attachment lasts a lifetime!

Chapter 26
Time Out

Time Out is a very powerful form of punishment that lets children know their behavior was so inappropriate they need to be alone for a while.

HOW TO USE TIME OUT

#1

Give the child one warning.
Tell the child if he continues to misbehave, he'll have to go to Time Out.

#2

If the child refuses to go, use minimal force and guide him to the Time Out area.

#3

Ignore all comments from the child that he'll never misbehave again.

#4

Tell the child how long Time Out will last.

#5

Remind the child that Time Out begins when the child is quiet.

#6

After the Time Out is over, redirect the child to appropriate behavior.

Try this ...

1. Discuss with your child Time Out as a punishment for behavior.
2. Explain to your child the rules of Time Out.
3. Have your child practice taking a Time Out.
4. Mention that Time Out will only be used to help children learn right from wrong.

Chapter 27
Child Proofing Your House from Danger

WHY CHILD PROOF?

Young children love to explore their environment.

It is natural for children to explore. They are curious.

Exploring their environment is important for their brains to develop.

They love to touch, grab, pull and eat just about anything around them.

Young children are not aware of what is safe to play with and what is harmful.

Child proofing the house prevents children from being harmed while they explore.

Child proofing your house keeps parents from constantly saying "NO" to all the things young children are discovering.

A house that is child proofed allows parents and their young children to build a strong attachment.

IS YOUR HOUSE CHILDPROOFED?

If you are wondering if your house is child proofed, here are some things you can do:

Crawl around your house on your hands and knees pretending you're a toddler.

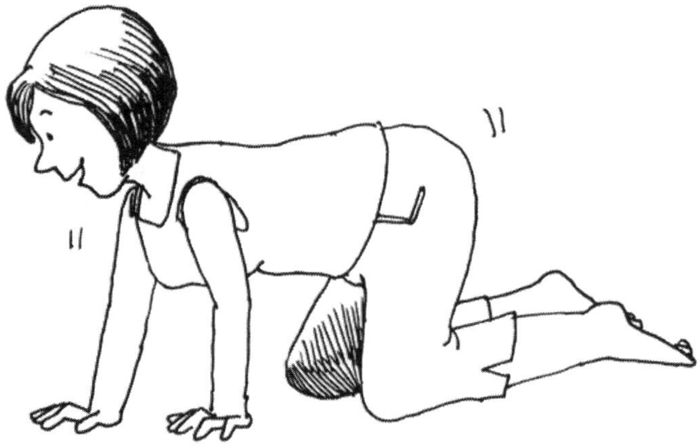

If you can grab something, so can your toddler.

If you can put something in the outlet, so can your child.

If you can put something in your mouth, so can your child.

If you can open a drawer, so can your child.

Place all the things you can grab, pull, open and eat out of reach.

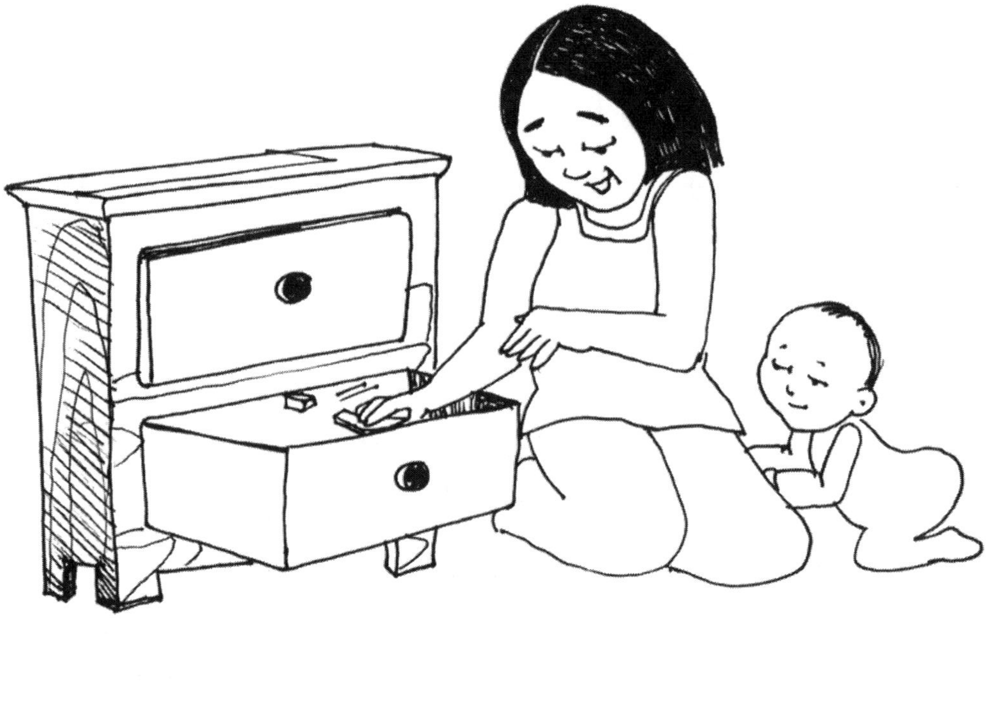

Put locks on all drawers within the reach of your child.

Cover all electric sockets.

A very effective way of child proofing your home is to watch your child explore. Walk behind your child and notice the things your child notices.

COMMON DANGERS TO CHILDREN

Paint chips

Many older homes have lead-based paint which can be toxic. Remove paint chips from wall and floor.

Cigarette butts

Nicotine can kill a child if eaten. Smoke outside away from your children and dispose of cigarette butts appropriately.

Lighters and matches

cause burns which are common injuries for preschoolers. Put all lighters and matches safely away.

Plants

Some can be poisonous. Put plants up high, out of reach.

Open containers of beer and alcohol are tempting for a child to drink which can cause liver and brain damage. Never leave open containers of alcohol where children can reach them.

Cat and dog food, or litter boxes with animal waste are dangerous if swallowed or can result in choking. Put litter boxes in enclosed rooms and animal food up and away from children.

Open stairways are dangerous for children who can easily fall and receive serious injuries. Place safety gates up by stairways and other dangerous areas.

Any toddler left alone without supervision in the house is a potential accident just waiting to happen.

Young children need <u>constant supervision</u>.

Try this ...
Get down on your hands and knees, crawl around and view the house as your child does. What you can touch, pull, grab or bite, so can your child. Move tempting objects out of the way.

Chapter 28

Verbal & Physical Redirection

Redirection is used to help children learn appropriate behavior, prevent injury, promote safe exploration, and prevent the constant threat of punishments.

VERBAL REDIRECTION ...

... redirects a child's behavior by stating **what not to do** followed by **what to do instead**.

"No standing in the tubby. Sit please."

"Don't play with the scissors. You could get hurt. Here's a toy to play with instead."

Threats are NOT appropriate ways to use verbal redirection.

Wrong ...

"Billy, you get your coat on right now or you'll get the spanking of your lifetime!"

Right ...

"Billy, in 10 minutes we are leaving to go to grandma's. I expect that you will be ready to go. Thanks for cooperating."

PHYSICAL REDIRECTION ...

... redirects children from dangerous situations or activities to safer, more appropriate ones. Electric sockets, climbing up and down stairs, and putting things in their mouths, are just some of the ways children can be injured.

"That's an oweee, honey! Come on sweetie, let's play with your toys instead."

Verbal and physical redirection work best when used together!

> **Try this ...**
> Find situations in your home where you can use verbal and physical redirection instead of spanking or yelling at your children. Describe the situation. How did you handle it?

Chapter 29
Establishing Nurturing Parenting Routines

Nurturing Parenting Routines provide children and parents with a consistent, predictable and caring way of family life.

NURTURING ROUTINES HAVE FOUR IMPORTANT FEATURES:

#1

Feelings of trust and security.

#2

Demonstrating caring for oneself and for others.

#3

A strong sense of
"Personal Power."

#4

Feelings of
positive self-worth.

NURTURING PARENTING ROUTINES

There are several important practices
that go into establishing
Nurturing Parenting Routines:

- Gentle touch
- Praising your child
- Happy, pleasant facial expressions
- Having a sense of caring
- Having fun and a sense of humor

Try this ...
Spend time each day playing, reading, talking to and massaging your children.

Chapter 30

Nurturing Parenting Diapering and Dressing Routine

Establishing a nurturing Diapering and Dressing Time Routine is important because ...

- Children learn cooperation.
- Children develop their autonomy.
- Children develop their self-worth.

STEPS IN ESTABLISHING A NURTURING PARENTING DIAPERING AND DRESSING ROUTINE:

#1

Let your children have input into what they will wear for the day.

#2

Allow your children to do the things they can do by themselves without any help from you.

#3

Assist your children in getting dressed when necessary, but allow them to still take the lead.

#4

Take the lead in helping your children get dressed by doing the things they are unable to do.

Make diapering and dressing a time for you and your children to bond.

Try this ...

Practice a Nurturing Diapering and Dressing Routine with your children each day.

Chapter 31

Nurturing Parenting Feeding Time Routine

Establishing a Nurturing Feeding Time
is important because ...

- Eating is a very pleasurable time.
- Children learn a way to care for themselves.
- Early food habits can last a lifetime

STEPS IN ESTABLISHING A NURTURING PARENTING FEEDING TIME ROUTINE:

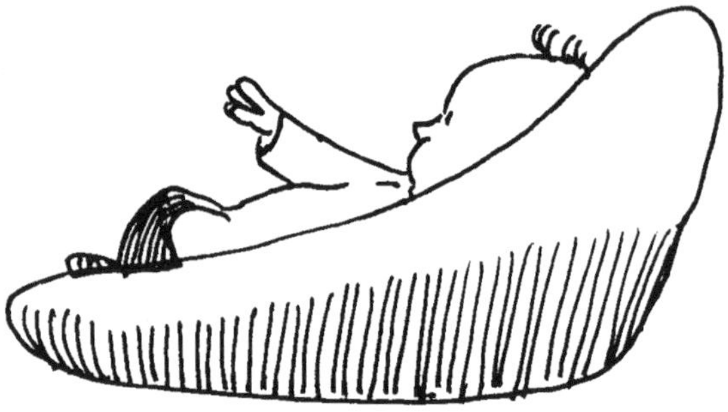

#1

Provide your child with a comfortable eating environment.

#2

Allow your child to reject certain foods when appropriate.

#3

Reinforce personal choice in eating.

#4

Try to get children to think of food as something they want, not something they need to reject.

#5

Encourage your child to begin to feed himself around nine to ten months.

#6

Encourage your child to use a spoon.

#7

Don't worry about table manners.

#8

Praise your child!

Mealtimes together as a family can have lasting positive memories!

Try this ...
Practice a Nurturing Diapering and Dressing Routine with your children each day.

Chapter 32
Feeding Your Children Nutritious Foods

Nutritious Foods for Children – Quick and Easy

Here are some ideas for snacks and means for your little ones. Be creative and add your own ideas!

Vegetable and Fruit Group

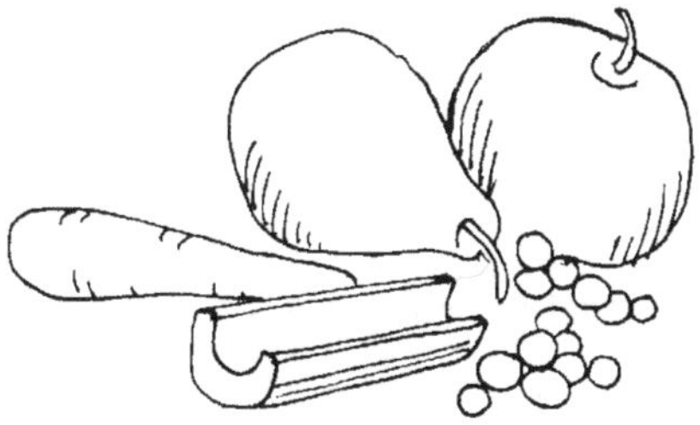

- Apples, peaches, pears, grapes, etc.
- Raw vegetable sticks or pieces (radishes, celery, cauliflower, green onions, zucchini, green peppers, carrots, cucumbers - even parsnips!).
- Dried apricots, raisins, prunes.
- Canned fruits or fruit juices kept chilled in the refrigerator.
- Mini-kabobs of bite-sized fruit chunks, strung on pretzel sticks.
- Banana chunks dipped in orange juice. Shake in a bag with chopped peanuts. Spear on pretzel sticks.
- Celery stuffed with cottage cheese, cheese spread or peanut butter.
- Juice cubes you make by freezing fruit juices in an ice cube tray.
- Tomato half, sprinkled with breadcrumbs, Parmesan or grated cheddar cheese and broiled.
- Creative salads of lettuce, raw spinach and other fresh vegetables, fruits, meats, eggs, or seafood.

Bread and Cereal Group

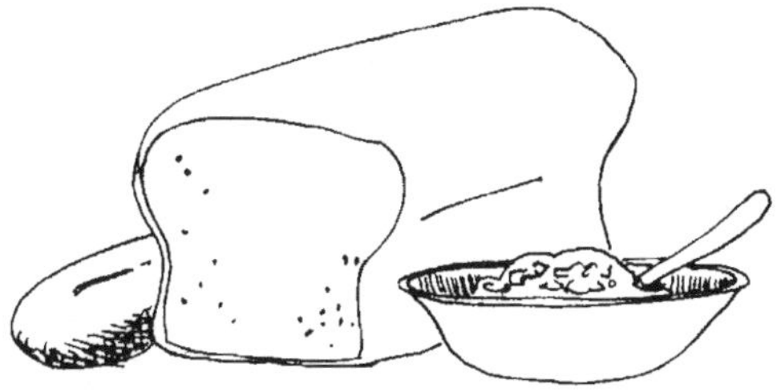

- Raisin bread toasted and spread with peanut butter.
- Sandwiches using a variety of breads - raisin, cracked wheat, pumpernickel, rye, black.
- Date-nut roll or brown bread spread with cream cheese.
- English muffins, served open-faced sandwiches such as hot roast beef or turkey, chicken salad, sloppy joes.
- Individual pizzas. Top English muffin halves with cheese slices, tomato sauce and oregano, and broil.
- Waffles topped with whipped topping and strawberries.
- Wheat or rye crackers topped with herb-seasoned cottage cheese, cheese or meat spread, or peanut butter.
- Graham crackers and milk.
- Ready-to-eat cereals right out of the box - provide cereals low in sugar.
- Ice cream or pudding, sprinkled with crisp cereals or wheat germ.

Meat, Poultry, Fish and Beans Group

- Nuts, sesame seeds, or toasted sunflower seeds.
- Sandwich spread of peanut butter combined with raisins or chopped dates.
- Peanut butter and honey spread on an English muffin, sprinkled with chopped walnuts, and heated under the broiler.
- Grilled open-faced peanut butter and mashed banana sandwich.
- Tomatoes stuffed with egg salad.
- Melon wedges topped with thinly sliced ham.
- Sandwich of cheese, meat, tomato, onion, and lettuce.
- Antipasto of tuna, shrimp, anchovies, hard cooked eggs and assorted vegetables.
- Leftover poultry or meat - as is, or chopped into a sandwich spread.
- Bite-sized cubes of broiled beef.

Milk and Cheese Group

- Milk shakes with mashed fresh berries or bananas.
- Parfait of cottage cheese, yogurt, or ice milk combined with fruit, sprinkled with chopped nuts, wheat germ, or crisp cereal.
- Dips for vegetable sticks. For fewer calories, substitute cottage cheese or plain yogurt for sour cream and mayonnaise in preparing dips.
- Fruit-flavored yogurt.
- Cheese cubes, or cheese cubes speared with pretzel sticks, or alternated with mandarin orange sections on a toothpick.
- Custard or pudding.
- Ice milk sundae, topped with fresh canned, or frozen fruits.

Tips for Cooking with Children

You are the model; don't let your likes and dislikes influence the selection of food experiences.

1. Offer a variety of wholesome foods to your children.
2. Allow children to see, smell, feel, and taste the food at different stages of preparation. Compare colors and textures, shapes and sizes.
3. Choose simple cooking experiences first.
4. Develop "picture recipes," including utensils and illustrated measurement of ingredients.
5. Review the recipe and all directions before beginning a food activity.
6. Have all utensils ready ahead of time.
7. Sanitation: Does everyone have clean hands? Wash hands and work surface before starting. Explain what to do if your child has to sneeze or cough.
8. Teach awareness of sharp objects and hot surfaces. Children use knives and graters only under close supervision.

Chapter 33

Nurturing Parenting Bath Time Routine

STEPS IN ESTABLISHING A NURTURING PARENTING BATH TIME ROUTINE:

#1

Make bath time sound like a fun time!

#2

With parental supervision, let your child turn on the water and fill the tub making sure the water is a safe temperature.

#3

Encourage your child to play in the tub using safe tubby toys.

#4

Encourage your child to get to know their body.

#5

It's okay for parents and young children to share tubby time!

#6

Make the experience of tubby time enjoyable:

- Use mild soaps and shampoos.
- Place a mat on the bottom of the tub to prevent accidental slipping.
- Protect against accidents by placing a foam rubber guard over the water spout.
- Get each of your children their own towel and their own robe to wear after taking a bath.

#7

Make tubby time a routine of the day.

#8

Help children step out of the tub onto a dry towel or rug.

#9

Help your child dry off and use the time to have fun!

#10

Finish the bath time by rubbing lotion on your child!

Try this ...
Practice a Nurturing Bath Time Routine with each of your children.

Chapter 34

Sexually Transmitted Diseases (STDs), HIV and AIDS

- STDs are sexually transmitted diseases.
- HIV or Human Immunodeficiency Virus is a STD which is the base infection for AIDS.
- Genital herpes is a common STD. Many people mistake it for a skin irritation.
- Chlamydia is a curable sexually transmitted infection caused by bacteria. Chlamydia can be passed on during oral, vaginal or anal sexual contact.
- Crabs are parasites that live on the pubic hair in the genital area.
- Gonorrhea is a treatable bacterial infection of the penis, vagina or anus that causes pain or a burning feeling as well as a pus-like discharge. Gonorrhea is also called the clap.
- Hepatitis is a STD that affects the liver.
- Genital warts are a virus that affects the skin in the genital area, as well as a female's cervix.
- Syphilis is a treatable bacterial infection that can spread throughout the body and affect the heart, brain and nerves.
- Vaginitis is caused by different germs including yeast and trichomoniases. It is an infection of the vagina resulting in itching, burning, vaginal discharge and an odd odor.

How is HIV Spread?

HIV is spread from one person to another through certain body fluids. These fluids include blood and blood products, semen (sperm), fluid from the vagina, and breast milk. The following are ways HIV can be spread:

- By sexual intercourse (vaginal, anal, or oral) with a person who is HIV infected.
- Through contact with an infected person's blood.
- To a baby by his or her HIV-infected mother.
- Through blood or blood products from blood transfusions, organ transplants, or artificial insemination.

Teaching Your Young Child About HIV and AIDS

Children need to learn about HIV and AIDS at a very early age. By the time your children are 3 or 4 years old, make sure you have clearly explained the following to them:

- They should never touch anyone else's blood or open sores.
- They should never touch needles or syringes.
- If they see someone who is bleeding or if they find a needle or a syringe, they should tell an adult.
- AIDS cannot be caught by playing with HIV-infected children.

By grade-school age, your child should begin to have a better understanding of illness and body parts. They should begin to learn about how HIV can and cannot be spread.

What are the Symptoms of AIDS?

Symptoms of diseases associated with AIDS may include:

- Swelling or hardening of glands located in the throat, groin, or armpit;
- The appearance of hard, discolored or purplish growths on the skin or inside the mouth;
- The appearance of a thick, whitish coating on the tongue or mouth, called thrush, which may also be accompanied by a sore throat;
- Increasing shortness of breath;
- Periods of continued deep, dry coughing that are not due to other illnesses or to smoking;
- Recurring fevers and/or night sweats;
- Rapid loss of more than 10 pounds of weight that is not due to increased physical exercise or dieting;
- Bruising more easily than normal;
- Unexplained bleeding from growths on the skin, from mucous membranes or from any opening in the body;
- Repeated occurrences of diarrhea.

Whether or not such symptoms prove to be AIDS related, a doctor should be consulted if any of these symptoms occur.

How Can People Avoid Getting AIDS?

- When having sex, follow safer sex guidelines - and always use condoms.
- Know your partner's health status and whether or not he or she has other sex partners;
- Do not exchange bodily fluids (blood and semen);

- Limit the number of sex partners (preferable to one person who has done the same);
- Never share needles to inject drugs (boiling does not guarantee sterility)
- Do not share toothbrushes, razors, or other personal items that could be contaminated with blood;
- Maintain a strong immune system: eat well, get enough rest and exercise, avoid recreational and illicit drugs, avoid heavy use of alcohol, have regular medical check-ups.

People with HIV are at risk for AIDS and people who carry the AIDS virus must not donate blood, plasma, sperm, body organs or other tissues.

How Do Women Get AIDS?

Like men, women can get AIDS by sharing needles with HIV drug users or by having sexual intercourse involving exchange of bodily fluids with a person who has AIDS or who is infected with the AIDS virus. A few women have developed AIDS following transfusions of contaminated blood.

Any pregnant woman who knows or thinks she may carry the virus should immediately consult a health care provider who is knowledgeable about AIDS, as the AIDS virus is very likely to spread from her to the fetus during pregnancy. It is also important to consult a health care provider if her partner has AIDS, if she or her partner is an HIV drug user or if either is having other sexual relationships.

Is There a Test to Determine if a Person Has Been Exposed to Aids?

Blood tests are available through private physicians, hospital clinics and blood banks, as well as most local, state and federal health departments. The tests are designed to detect antibodies to AIDS. The presence of AIDS antibodies in a person's blood means that they have been exposed to the AIDS virus, but does not mean that the person has, or will have, AIDS. Though they are highly accurate, AIDS antibody tests can only be reliable in detecting infections that are more than four months old.

Who Should be Tested for Antibodies to Aids?

Confidential testing may be appropriate for people at risk for AIDS and/or for their partners who:

- Are considering parenthood;
- Are considering enlistment in the armed forces;
- Have been exclusively monogamous for a number of years and wish to disregard safer sex guidelines.

There are several considerations to make before deciding to be tested for antibodies to AIDS:

- Testing positive for AIDS antibodies does not mean that a person has, or will develop, AIDS;

- Test results cannot distinguish persons who have developed an immunity to AIDS from those who have not;
- Birth control pills, alcoholism, and other factors may cause false positive results indicating infection when there is none.

How is AIDS Treated?

Currently, there are no medicines that can cure AIDS and, for now, there is no vaccine to prevent it.

People with AIDS not only require the most advanced medicines and chemical therapies, they also require psychologically positive environments. The latest medical research indicates that there is a direct relationship between a person's psychological outlook and the function of his or her immune system.

Members of the community need to realize that no one has ever contracted AIDS in any way other than those listed previously.

Taken from Planned Parenthood of America and the American Academy of Pediatrics.

Chapter 35

Developing Children's Sexual Self-Worth

Sexual self-worth is the respect children have for their own bodies.

Children need to have a positive sexual self-worth to develop healthy perceptions about their bodies.

The following are ideas for building the positive sexual self-worth in children:

Teach children correct names for sexual body parts: penis, testicles, vagina, breasts and buttocks (butt or bottom are acceptable).

Nudity during bath times is a good way to teach children proper names for genitals.

Be honest. When children ask questions about body parts, provide a truthful response that is age appropriate.

Teach children about the different types of touch: gentle, hurting and scary. When children learn about the different types of touch, they can better recognize and reject unwanted touch.

Respect personal space. Ask children if they want help zipping a zipper, or blowing their nose rather than just invading their personal space.

Respect's children's right to say "NO." When children can say "no" to unwanted touch, they can feel more confident in protecting their body.

The following are ideas for building sexual self-worth in adults:

Accept yourself and your body. It is the body you have.

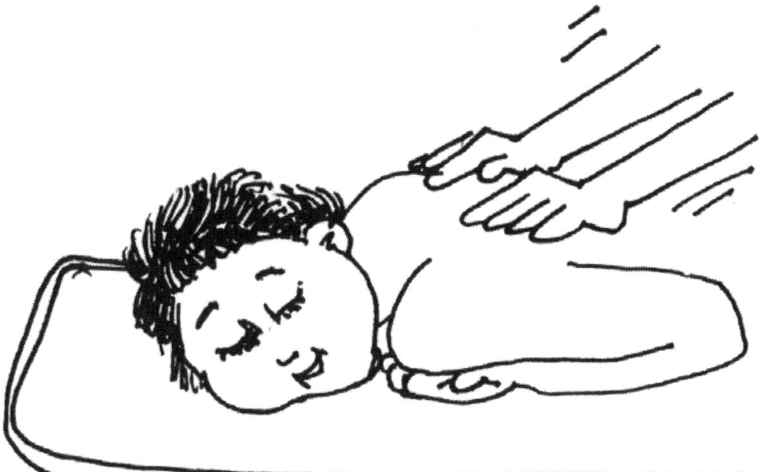

Schedule times to get massages. Massages reduce stress, and can help adults feel better about their bodies.

Take care of your body. Exercise, take walks, play sports. When your body feels good, you feel good.

Become aware of the beliefs you learned as a child about your body and sex. Becoming aware is the first step in changing unwanted beliefs.

Try this ...
List three things you can do to improve your own sexual self-worth. Then list three things you can do to improve your children's sexual-self worth. Are they the same or different?

Chapter 36

Nurturing Parenting Bed Time Routine

Time Facts:

- Infants are born with irregular sleep cycles which take almost 6 months to mature.
- Newborns sleep an average of 16 to 17 hours per day.
- Babies sleep in stages:

  First Stage: Deep Sleep - the eyelids are firmly closed and there is little movement.

  Second Stage: Light Sleep or Slow Waking Up - the baby makes light whimpers, has irregular breathing, and her eyes appear to be moving under the eyelids.

  Third Stage: Awake Stage - eyes are open and baby is responsive

STEPS IN ESTABLISHING A NURTURING PARENTING BED TIME ROUTINE:

#1

Identify a consistent time your child will be going to bed.

#2

Make a nice, relaxing bath time part of the night time routine for going to bed.

#3

Dress your child in clothes especially for bed time.

#4

Help your child get dressed for sleep in their bedroom, not in other rooms of the house.

#5

Have your child brush their teeth every night as part of the nurturing bed time routine.

#6

Spend time with your child reading stories.

#7

Choose bed time stories that are happy and pleasing - books which add comfort, not discomfort.

#8

When you're finished reading, tell your child it's time to go to bed.

#9

Tuck your child in and sing a song or tell your child a "power story" by highlighting all their efforts or accomplishments of the day!

#10

If your child should begin to cry during the night, go into their room and find out what the problem is.

Try this ...
Practice a Nurturing Bed Time Routine with each of your children.

Chapter 37

Understanding and Handling Stress

Bad Stress
(or Distress) ...
When the demands of life cause great suffering and pain.

Good Stress ...
The emotional response to the normal demands of life.

HOW TO HANDLE STRESS ...

Take hot baths.

Exercise.

Learn to relax.

Eat healthy foods.

Have a positive attitude and outlook.

Set realistic expectations for yourself.

Feel good about yourself.

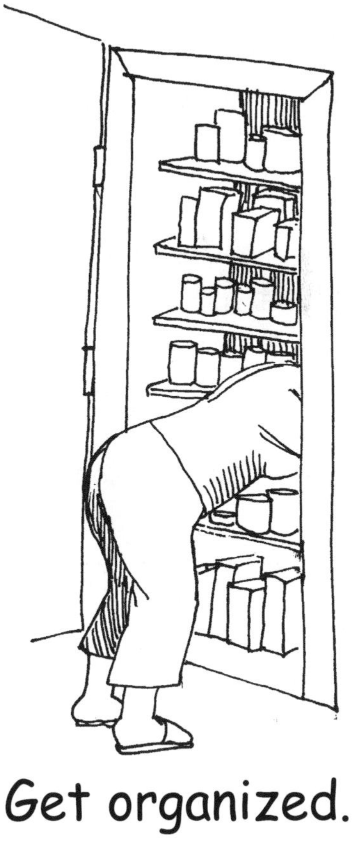

Get organized.

Have friends!

Have a sense of humor!

Try this ...

1. Identify five stressors (things that cause stress) in your life: ____________________

   ____

2. Make a plan for how you can reduce or prevent these stressors from affecting the quality of your life.

3. Develop a plan to cope with the stressors you can't change.

4. Identify five stressors in your children's lives: ______________________________

   ____

   ____

5. What can you do to help your children reduce their stress? ____________________

   ____

Chapter 38
Helping Children Manage Their Behavior

As children get older, they become more capable!

Helping children manage their own behavior teaches them responsibility and builds their own self-worth.

THE FOLLOWING ARE GOOD WAYS TO HELP CHILDREN MANAGE THEIR BEHAVIOR:

#1

Give children choices.

#2

Give children consequences for their choices.

(Example:)

Cleaned room = Play outside later.

Room not cleaned = Stay in until room is cleaned.

#3

Offer transition time between activities.

(Example:)

"Karen, you can read for five more minutes and then it's time to come in for supper."

#4

Problem solve solutions to problems together.

#5

At times, negotiate and compromise.

#6
Ask "What can you do instead"?

#7
Ask "What have you learned"?

Try this ...
Use the techniques to help children manage their behavior. What techniques did you use? Were they successful?

Chapter 39

Ignoring as a Parenting Technique

Ignoring is a parenting technique to reduce or stop children's behaviors that parents find annoying.

Ignoring means not paying any attention to your child when the annoying behavior is occurring.

Ignoring does not mean criticizing, threatening or hitting your child.

Ignoring is not appropriate to use when children are experiencing an emergency or are hurting others.

Never ignore children when they may get injured.

Never ignore behavior when property is purposefully damaged, like throwing and breaking toys.

BEFORE YOU USE IGNORING ...

1. Decide what behavior you want to see instead.

2. Be sure you can tolerate the behavior.

3. Make sure you can ignore the behavior 100% of the time.

4. Try re-directing the behavior.

5. Try some preventive planning to avoid a bad time.

HOW TO USE IGNORING ...

1. Discuss with your child behaviors you will ignore.

2. When behavior occurs, give the child one warning.

3. When behavior occurs, ignore it 100% of the time.

4. Keep ignoring even as long as the behavior occurs.

5. Make sure grandparents, brothers, sisters ignore the behavior as well.

6. **Praise the child** immediately after the behavior stops.

Remember to **ignore the behavior and not the child.**

Try this ...

1. Discuss with your child how irritating certain behaviors can be. List these behaviors in your Family Rules, making sure you also list the wanted, desirable behaviors.
2. Practice using the technique of Ignoring with your children. When did it work? When did it not work?

Chapter 40

Nurturing Parenting Toilet Training

Before you start to teach your child how to use the toilet, there are some important things that must be checked first.

IS YOUR CHILD READY?

Age

Children should be at least 2 years old before you begin potty training.

Gender

Boys generally take longer to be potty trained than girls.

Muscle Control

Can your child pull their pants up and down? Does he have good muscle control?

Physical Development

Is your child's diaper dry after napping? When peeing, is there a steady flow of urine?

IS YOUR CHILD READY?

Communication

Does your child make some sound, facial expression or physical movement to let you know he has to go?

Follow Verbal Instructions

Give your child verbal instructions and see if he can follow through.

Desire

Lastly, you have to determine whether or not your child has the desire to learn.

BEFORE YOU BEGIN YOUR TEACHING ...

Words to Use

Keep the words simple so a child can say them.

Model the Appropriate Behavior

Let the child see you and other family members using the bathroom.

Buy a Potty Chair

Encourage your child to see it, play with it, and become familiar with it before he begins to use it.

Buy Training Pants

Help him learn to pull them up and pull them down.

TEACHING POTTY TRAINING

- **Pick a good day** to begin. Plan to set aside the entire day for helping and supporting your child.

- **Stay with your child** in the bathroom while he is having a bowel movement.

- **Praise his efforts.** It might take some children awhile to do their bowel movement. Don't pressure your child, support him.

- Teach your child **how to wipe** him/herself.

- Teach boys and girls to **wash their hands** after using the toilet.

- Accidents will happen. **Don't make a big deal about accidents.** Make a big deal when your child uses the potty successfully!

SOME FINAL POINTS TO REMEMBER ...

NEVER, **use punishment** in teaching your child to use the potty, and ...

The greatest single outcome that a child can learn from the whole experience of toilet teaching is **positive regard for him or herself** as a boy or girl.

Keep this fact in mind as you're helping your child learn to use the potty.

Try this ...
If appropriate, practice potty training your child using the techniques and steps presented in this chapter. How did it go?

Chapter 41
Understanding and Expressing Your Anger

Anger, like all feelings and thoughts, has ENERGY!
It is the **way** we express the energy that is either ...

Appropriate ... ... or **Inappropriate**

Anger is a Feeling of Discomfort.

Anger develops when we have been emotionally hurt, keep the hurt feelings inside and don't express them.

Keeping the hurt feelings inside is like stepping on a spring and trying to hold it down.

It's difficult to hold in hurt feelings and when they're finally expressed (stepping off the spring) they usually come out as anger.

The more we keep our feelings of hurt inside, the greater our anger grows.

Anger can grow and become uncontrollable.

When this happens, anger becomes RAGE!
People who feel rage generally get violent, hurt themselves and others, and destroy things.

In rage, people blame others for their anger when it really belongs to them.

Sometimes when people hide their feelings of hurt and anger, they become depressed.

Feeling depressed is often the result of not expressing our anger.

Hitting children is NOT an appropriate way to handle anger.

Getting drunk is NOT an appropriate way to handle anger.

When we appropriately express our anger, we feel better!

APPROPRIATE WAYS TO HANDLE ANGER ...

Find non-violent ways to express anger energy.

Make a pledge to yourself, your family, and others that you will find appropriate ways to express your anger.

To prevent feelings of anger, express your hurt when you feel it ... don't keep it inside!

Finally, make friends with your anger ...

... by taking responsibility for your angry feelings!

Try this ...

1. Identify people, situations or events that create feelings of anger in you: ____________
   ____
2. How do you handle your feelings of anger? ____________________
   ____
3. Are there better ways to express your anger? ____________________
4. What can you do to prevent feeling angry? ____________________
   ____
   ____

Chapter 42
Teaching Children to Express Their Anger

There are three rules to follow in expressing anger:

Rule #1

Do Respect Yourself - Don't Hurt Yourself

Rule #2

Do Respect Others - Don't Hurt Others

Rule #3

Do Respect the Environment - Don't Destroy the Environment

DON'T teach children to hit a pillow or punching bag ...

... hitting **something** can easily turn into hitting **someone**.

DO role model appropriate ways to release anger energy ...

... children learn by watching parents behave!

DON'T tell children to keep their anger inside ...

... their anger will grow so big they won't be able to handle it

DO help children find appropriate ways to express their anger.

DON'T tell children they can't express their anger...

DO brainstorm with children appropriate ways they can express their anger ...

... Let them come up with the right way!

DON'T ignore children when they are feeling anger ...

DO talk to them and ask them what is troubling them.

DON'T tell children not to cry ...

DO tell children that crying can be a very good thing to do when they are feeling hurt.

NEVER, EVER HURT ANIMALS!

Hurting animals is **NOT a phase** kids go through ...

... Hurting animals is a sign of a **child in TROUBLE**!

Children and adults who hurt animals need HELP!

Try this ...
Help your children handle their anger in appropriate ways.

Chapter 43
Communicating Thoughts and Feelings

The key to healthy communication is to communicate your thoughts and feelings in a way that does not purposefully hurt someone, or encourage someone to think less of themselves.

We are responsible for the way we feel.

I Statements are expressions about me and are clear statements about how I feel, think or need.

"I am angry."
"I need a hug."
"I want some quiet time."

You Messages are about someone else. When you use You Messages to put the **blame** on someone else, you do not accept responsibility for your own feelings, thoughts or needs.

"You make me angry."
"He made me feel upset."
"She made me feel sad."

Appropriate Use of YOU Messages

You Messages are used appropriately in five ways:

1. **To give choices.**

   "Carson, you have a choice. You can clean your room now, or you can clean your room later. However, if your room is not cleaned by 6:00 p.m., you can't watch TV tonight. It's your choice."

2. **To give praise.**

   "You must feel very proud."
   "You did that so well!"

3. To gain clarification.

"You don't seem to like the movie."

4. To ask questions.

"Are you hungry?"

5. To reflect feelings.

"Darlinda, you seem to be feeling very sad."

Try this ...
Practice using **I Statements** and not blaming **You Messages** when communicating your thoughts and feelings. Make a list of the times you normally would have used blaming You Messages but used I Statements instead. What differences did you notice in you and the others?

Chapter 44
Criticism and Confrontation

Communication is an important part of all relationships. There are two ways to tell other people something about them or what they did ...

... Criticism and Confrontation.

Criticism is what we have to say to another person WITHOUT regard to their feelings.

Confrontation is what we have to say to another person WITH regard to their feelings.

Criticism uses comments that ...

... are meant to hurt another person's feelings.

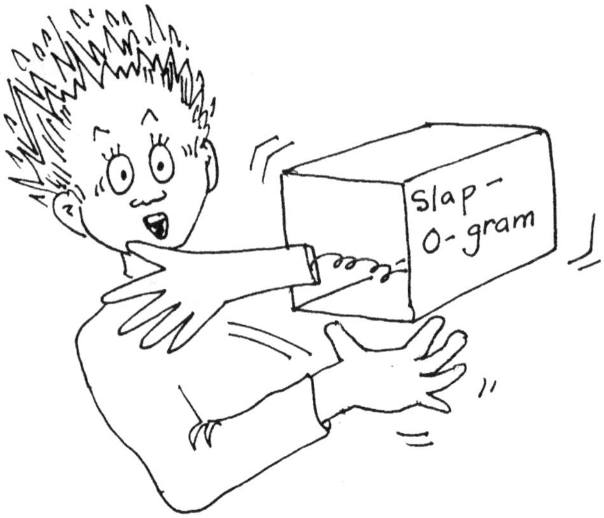

... can be verbal abuse -- it's like slapping a person in the face with words.

... tear down self worth.

... blame others for the way we feel.

... push people to become defensive and fight back.

... fuel angry feelings in others.

Confrontation uses comments that ...

... communicate respect for others.

... help others listen to what you have to say.

... provide useful information.

... promote a friendship.

... encourage others to change.

... are given from the heart.

EXAMPLES OF CRITICISM:

"You are a lazy slob. Look at this room. Are you a pig?"

"Your breath smells like you ate a dead skunk!"

"You look like a tramp with all that make-up on!"

EXAMPLES OF CONFRONTATION:

"This room needs to be cleaned. I'm disappointed you aren't following our family rules."

"Your breath needs some mouth wash."

"I think the amount of make-up you're wearing hides your real beauty."

TIPS TO CONFRONT AND NOT CRITICIZE:

1. Be calm.
2. Stay in the present moment and don't bring up the past.

3. Choose only to talk about one issue at a time.
4. Own your feelings. No blaming.
5. Listen to the other person.
6. Don't argue at night or in bed.
7. Discuss the issues when they happen. Don't save them up.
8. Problem solve and agree upon a solution.

Try this ...
Instead of criticizing, try confronting another person. Notice the difference in style. Was it successful?

Chapter 45
Families and Alcohol Abuse

Drug and alcohol abuse destroy healthy families.

The following questions are meant to increase your awareness of alcohol abuse in your family. Answer each question **Yes, No,** or **Don't Know**.

Question	Yes	No	Don't Know
1. Do you feel you have a drinking problem?			
2. Do you feel others in your family have a drinking problem?			
3. Do you often drink to feel better?			
4. Do you drink to "get through the day?"			
5. Have you had fights with friends or family about YOUR drinking?			
6. Have you had fights with friends or family about a FAMILY MEMBER drinking?			
7. Have YOU ever tried to stop drinking but couldn't?			
8. Has a FAMILY MEMBER ever tried stop drinking but couldn't?			
9. Have YOU ever been driving while drunk?			
10. Has a FAMILY MEMBER ever been driving while drunk?			
11. Have YOU ever sought help to stop your drinking?			
12. Has a FAMILY MEMBER ever sought help to stop drinking?			

Answering **Yes** to any of the questions provides you awareness and perhaps the need to seek professional help for you or a family member.

Chapter 46
Keeping Kids Drug Free

KEEPING CHILDREN DRUG FREE IS NOT IMPOSSIBLE. HERE IS OUR 12 STEP PROGRAM:

#1

Demonstrate caring.

#2

Talk to your children about their day and activities.

#3

Raise children without any violence.

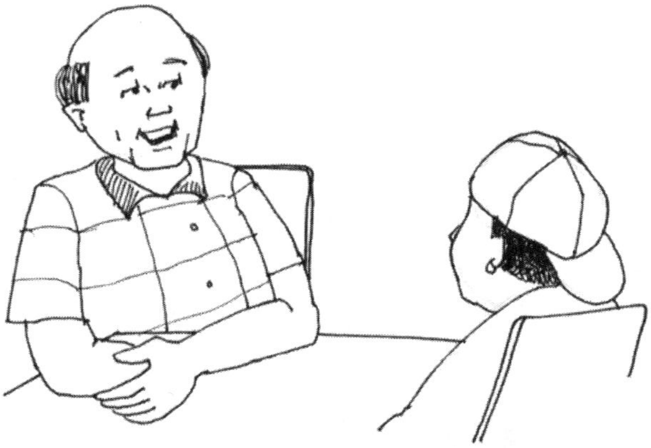

#4

Discuss drugs, their dangers and ways to avoid them WITH your children not TO your children.

#5

If you drink, model appropriate drinking.

#6

No drinking under the age of 21 means NO drinking.

#7

Do not have, use or allow illegal drugs in your home.

#8

Don't back off from your values. Stand your ground.

#9

Say "yes" to a healthy lifestyle.

#10

Talk with and listen to your children.

#11
Have fun as a family.

#12
Know your kids friends!

Try this ...
Use the ideas mentioned in this chapter to help keep your kids drug-free.

Chapter 47

How to Protect Our Children

The basic philosophy of safety is that children have the right to be safe. Here are some tips for keeping your children safe.

Safety from PHYSICAL Harm

- Home
- Babysitters
- Cars
- Boyfriends
- Preschool & School
- Community and Peer Groups
- Strangers

Safety from EMOTIONAL Harm

Safety from SEXUAL Harm

Keeping Your Children Supervised

* Appreciation to Linda Christmas, Program Director of Family Matters, Monroe, Louisiana for her dedication to helping families and keeping kids safe. Your nurturing spirit will always be remembered.

Safety from PHYSICAL HARM addresses many areas:

Safety at HOME

Is your home child proofed?

- Are dangerous objects out of reach? Are small items like paper clips, rubber bands, pop tops from cans, tooth picks, safety pins, picked up off the floor and out of reach of children?

- Are heavy objects away from the edge of tables?

- Can children climb on chairs and get to dangerous objects?

- Is the cat litter box and pet food stored in out-of-the-way locations?

- Are electric sockets capped?

- Do your cabinets have safety locks?

- A good thing to do to make sure your home is safe is to crawl around on the floor. What you see and can reach is what your child can see and reach!

Safety in CARS

- Always use a **car safety seat**. Start with your baby's first ride home from the hospital.

- Always use car safety seats for children until they get big enough to sit in the back seat strapped in.

- Never place a child in a rear facing car seat in the front seat. The **air bags** can injure your child.

- The safest place for children to ride is the **back seat.**

- Set a good example and wear your **seat belt**.

- **Never leave your child unattended** in a car with the windows rolled up and the car running or parked.

Safety with BABY SITTERS

Knowing whom you are leaving your child with is important BEFORE leaving your child with anyone.

- **Get references** from other parents for baby sitters.

- **Invite the person over** while you are home and watch how your child is treated.

- Get to **meet the family of the baby sitter** BEFORE you leave your child.

- Make sure there are **emergency back-ups** for your babysitter. Leave names and phone numbers of relatives, neighbors, etc.

- **Never, ever leave your child with someone** if you do not feel 100% sure your child will be treated with respect and will not be harmed.

Safety with BOYFRIENDS

Boyfriends can be a safe or dangerous source of care for your child. Studies show that males are more likely to shake babies and young children than females. "Shaken Baby Syndrome" is the cause of many infant deaths.

- BEFORE leaving your child with your boyfriend, **observe how he handles your child** in your presence. How does he respond to your crying child?

- DO NOT leave your child with your boyfriend or anyone else who has a **drug and/or alcohol problem**. Children need caring, stable and reliable people as caregivers.

Safety in PRESCHOOL and SCHOOL SETTINGS

Children spend a lot of time at school. School is like having a job. Because children are going to be around many different adults and other children, here are some suggestions for keeping your child safe.

- **Meet your child's school teachers** and administrators. Make sure they know who you are.

- **Be a presence** in your child's school. Volunteer for lunchroom and playground duty. Become a teacher's aide.

- **Drop in without notice**, especially at the preschool level and observe how the school really operates.

- Check the **"physical punishment" policy** of your school. Make sure you tell teachers that your child is not to be hit.

- Pay attention to children with the reputation of being a **bully**. Does your school have an anti-bully policy in place?

- Pay attention to outsiders or older children hanging around the school and school parking lot. Communities have made schools a Drug Free zone. The school should be free from **drugs and gangs**.

- If your child is involved in **after-school activities**, get to know the teacher. Private lessons can be unsafe situations for children. If you can, be present. If not, ask your child what went on during every session. Unwillingness to talk about the session or not wanting to go back could be a sign that something is not right.

- Make it a policy that your child is **never alone with an adult**. Remember there is safety in numbers!

Safety in COMMUNITY SETTINGS and PEER GROUPS

Knowing where your child is and with whom is critical in keeping your child safe. Here are some suggestions for your child's safety:

- **Travel in pairs and groups.** Once again, there is safety in numbers.

- **Give your child a cell phone.** The ability to get help is critical for your child's safety. And, if the child is going to be late, or if travel arrangements have changed, have your child call you and let you know.

- **Know your child's friends.** Invite them over. Let your house be the place where everyone gathers!

- **Meet the parents** of your children's closest friends.

- Have your child **buddy up**. If walking to and from school is necessary, make sure your child walks with others on main, well lit and populated streets.

Safety from STRANGERS

Most children are taken, hurt or killed by people they know - not strangers.

- Create a **password** between you and your child. This password is used in emergencies. If a stranger says to your child that her parents have been hurt and she must come with him, have your child ask for the **password**. If the stranger cannot give the password, your child is not to go along, but to run away, start screaming, use the cell phone to check with you or run to another adult they know. **Teach your child that under no circumstances are they to go anywhere with people they do not know.** Use the password.

- **If children get lost**, teach them to "find a mommy" and say you are lost. Or look for someone in uniform like the police or fire fighter, etc and say you are lost. In a store, look for a salesperson or someone behind the cash register.

- **Teach your children to scream, yell, kick, and run if someone they do not know grabs them.** Most children are frightened and go along without fighting back or running away.

Safety from EMOTIONAL HARM

Safety from Emotional Harm especially relates to the Internet, video games, TV and the movies. Parental control is the best way to keep children safe.

- Sexual molestation occurs for many children who arrange meetings on the internet. Molesters use **e-mail, chat rooms and instant messaging** to get potential victims.

- **Harassment and bullying** can happen to a child in person, via E-mail or through cell phones. Such bullying is meant to bother the child, but can cause a lot of emotional distress.

- **Video games that have sexual and violent language and graphics** can confuse children into thinking that such actions are normal. Children learn violent behavior by experiencing it first hand, and also by watching violence in movies, on TV and in video games.

Parents can prevent emotional harm to their children and promote their emotional safety by observing Internet, computer games and cell phone use.

Safety from SEXUAL HARM

Safety from Sexual Harm is an ongoing concern. Studies show that 1 in 7 girls will be sexually approached on the Internet. Additionally, one in four women and one in six men report having experienced some form of sexual abuse in childhood. There are proven steps parents can use to protect their children.

- **Educate children about sex**, sexual body parts, and sexual abuse at an early but appropriate age in life.

- Most sexual abuse occurs with someone the child knows. **Be knowledgeable of who is with your children.**

- **Teach children to be assertive.** Teach them to use "no" when it comes to unwanted or sexual touch.

- **Teach children personal protective skills** such as screaming, yelling, running away, scratching if grabbed by a stranger.

- **Respect children's bodies.** Use proper terminology when referring to children's sexual body parts.

- **Keep open the communication** between you and your child. If your child cannot communicate with their parents and get factual and respectful communication, then the child is left to other, often-unreliable sources for information.

KEEPING YOUR CHILDREN SUPERVISED

Remember, children need to be supervised at all times.

Be aware of where your children are and what they're doing when you are:

- at work
- out with your friends
- on the phone
- cooking
- sleeping
- watching TV

Supervise your children or make sure they have adequate supervision when they are ...

- at the mall
- at the movies
- at a skating rink
- at a playground

Don't allow your children to play in an unsafe place or a place with no or inadequate supervision like ...

- in an unfenced yard
- at a lake
- in the park

Try this ...
Start using the safety tips offered in this Chapter. Which ones did you use? Did they work?

Chapter 48
Possessive and Violent Relationships

A loving relationship is **UNCONDITIONAL.**

A possessive and violent relationship is **CONDITIONAL.**

Many women remain in possessive and violent relationships because they ...

... see violence and abuse as common.

... witness abuse between parents.

... are not sure if the relationship is possessive.

... are afraid to date others.

WARNING SIGNS TO LOOK FOR:

- Your boy/girlfriend is **jealous**.

- They make **critical comments** about your appearance and your friends.

- They want you to **spend all your time with them**.

- You have **physical injuries**.
- You have **feelings of embarrassment**.

- You turn to **drugs** to cope.

Try this ...
If you are in a possessive and violent relationship, seek help. Call your local shelter for domestic violence, or 911. Your safety, health and life are valuable and you do not deserve to be mistreated by anyone.

Chapter 49

Smoking and My Child's Health

FACTS:

Pregnant women who smoke have an increased risk of having children born **premature**, or with **low birth weight**. Some children are born **dead**.

Children of women who smoke while pregnant have a higher risk of having **behavior problems**.

Teens that do poorly in school are more likely to smoke.

Depression also is a higher risk among people who smoke.

Women who smoke go into menopause earlier.

SECOND HAND SMOKE

Children can also suffer **health and behavior problems** from parents who smoke. This is called second hand smoke.

Secondhand smoke is a major cause in children's illnesses.

Secondhand smoke is linked to middle ear infections, asthma, and trouble breathing in children.

Parents are important role models. If they smoke it is likely their children will smoke.

To make sure your child is born healthy and stays healthy, don't smoke, or stop smoking.

Try this ...
If you smoke, make a serious plan for stopping. If others smoke in your home, or around you or your children, make the immediate space around you and your children a "smoke-free zone." Nurture yourself and your children by improving the health of you and your children.

Chapter 50

Problem Solving, Decision Making, Negotiation and Compromise

When parents and children both have different ideas on what to do, what to wear, when to come home, etc., people usually get tense. When this happens, the discussion often leads to arguments. This is where **Problem Solving and Decision Making** are useful.

PROBLEM SOLVING AND DECISION MAKING

Problem Solving: What to do when you have a problem but don't know what the solution is.

Decision Making: What you do when you know some possible solutions.

Solving problems can be something we do by ourselves or something we do as a family. To reach a point of action in solving problems, both personal and familial, certain steps need to be followed.

Steps for PROBLEM SOLVING

Step 1
Identify the problem. Write it down. Work on only one problem at a time.

Step 2
Whose problem is it? Is someone doing something you don't like but does not see it as a problem? Is the problem yours or someone else's?

Step 3

Talk with the person and discuss what you have tried to do to solve the problem.

Step 4

Write down a goal statement that both of you agree on. What would be the best solution to the problem? Be specific. Don't identify what you don't want to see; identify what you DO want to see.

Step 5

Brainstorm ways to make the solution work. Whether it's your problem or someone else's problem, come up with ways to make the solution work.

Step 6

Make a decision. Pick out your favorite three ideas and try them.

NEGOTIATION AND COMPROMISE

If problem solving doesn't work, then try to **Negotiate** and **Compromise**.

Steps for NEGOTIATION AND COMPROMISE:

Step 1

Determine if there is a **difference of opinion** between you and the other person.

Step 2

State your views and what you think the views of the other person are.

Step 3
Ask the person if your statement is correct.

Step 4
Offer a compromise and keep negotiating until an agreeable solution is reached.

Try this ...
Practice using problem solving, decision making, negotiating and compromising. What were the outcomes? Did it work?